Battle of Waterloo

A Short Account

Felicity McCullough

Series: Glimpses of the Past
Illustrated: Black and White

Copyright

Copyright 2015 My Lap Shop Publishers

All Rights Reserved

No part of this publication may be reproduced, stored in a retrieval system, or transmitted in any form or by any means, electronic, mechanical, photocopying, recording, scanning, or otherwise, without the prior written permission of the Publisher. Requests to the Publisher for permission should be addressed to:

My Lap Shop Publishers

91 Mayflower Street, Unit 222, Plymouth, Devon PL1 1SB, United Kingdom

Battle of Waterloo A Short Account

Published by:

My Lap Shop Publishers

91 Mayflower Street, Unit 222,
Plymouth, Devon PL1 1SB,
United Kingdom
Tel: +44 (0)871 560 5297
www.mylapshop.com

About My Lap Shop Publishers

First Edition June 2015

Black & White Paperback **ISBN:**

978-1-78165-074-5

Introduction

The book gives a brief account of the events surrounding the Battle of Waterloo and the key people involved.

It is hoped that you enjoy reading and learning about what happened two hundred years ago.

The information has been extracted from various historical sources and research.

The battle took place after Napoleon returned to power in France when a coalition of countries in Europe decided to declare war on him.

As you will discover, it was a very costly war in terms of lives lost.

Table of Illustrations

I King Louis XVIII of France 11
II Marshall Blücher 13
III Duke of Wellington 14
IV Henry Paget, 2nd Earl of Uxbridge 15
V Marshall Grouchy 18
VI Jean-de-Dieu Soult 19
VII Charlotte Lennox, Duchess of Richmond née Lady Charlotte Gordon 21
VIII August Neidhardt von Gneisenau Prussian Chief of Staff 25
IX Alexander Cavalié Mercer 27
X Jean-Baptiste Drouet, Comte d'Erlon 32
XI Lieutenant General Sir Thomas Picton 33
XII Napoléon Bonaparte 34
XIII Major-General Sir William Ponsonby 37
XIV Michel Ney, 1st Duc d'Elchingen, 1st Prince de la Moskowa 41
XV General Sir Peregrine Maitland 46
XVI HMS Bellerophon 51

Contents

Battle of Waterloo 1

A Short Account 1
Felicity McCullough 1
Series: Glimpses of the Past 1
Illustrated: Black and White 1

Copyright 2
Published by: 3
About My Lap Shop Publishers 3
Introduction 4
Table of Illustrations 5
Contents 6
Waterloo 9
The Seventh Coalition 9
War against Napoleon 10
King Louis XVIII of France 11
War 12
Gebhard Leberecht von Blücher 13
Belgium 13
Duke of Wellington 14
Lord Uxbridge, Marquise of Anglesey 15
Prussian Army 16
French Army 16
Emmanuel de Grouchy, 2ème Marquis de Grouchy 18
Jean-de-Dieu Soult 19
Conflict 20

Duchess of Richmond 21
The Ridge 21
Battle of Quatre Bras 22
Battle of Ligny 23
August Neidhardt von Gneisenau 25
Thunderstorm 26
Alexander Cavalié Mercer 27
La Belle Alliance 28
La Haye Sainte 29
Hougoumont 29
Jean-Baptiste Drouet, Comte d'Erlon 32
Thomas Picton 33
Napoleon at the Ridge 34
Charge of the Royal Scots Greys 35
Capture of the French Eagle 36
Major-General Sir William Ponsonby 37
The French Cavalry 39
The Square 39
Brest plate 40
Michel Ney 41
The final assault 43
The Rout 45
Sir Peregrine Maitland 46
Casualties 48
Asylum 49
HMS Bellerophon 51
About Felicity McCullough 53

Other Publications 54

Index	55
Published by:	59
About My Lap Shop Publishers	59

Waterloo

Two hundred years ago in 1814 Napoleon Bonaparte, Emperor of France, was ousted from power. He was exiled to the Island of Elba. When the British and French ships, guarding him were deployed elsewhere, he escaped and with loyal followers made plans to recapture Paris.

The Seventh Coalition

The Austrians, Russians, Prussians and the British were known as the Seventh Coalition, being involved during the previous Napoleonic Wars. The Seventh Coalition, were keen once Napoleon had been deposed, to redraw the boundaries of the European countries and were determined to re-carve Europe and to expand their own territories.

The European Seventh Coalition included Britain, Russia, Prussia, the Netherlands, Sweden, Austria, Spain, Portugal, Sardinia, and a number of German States, which had all joined the coalition, in order to defeat the French Emperor.

War against Napoleon

Britain financed getting rid of Napoleon and provided 40% of the troops. Britain never declared war on France. Britain declared war only against the man, Napoleon.

At the beginning of 1815 Napoleon fought to regain his power embarking on eliminating the enemies of France, culminating in the Battle of Waterloo.

Battle of Waterloo A Short Account

King Louis XVIII of France

I King Louis XVIII of France

King Louis 18th had been restored as King of France after Napoleon's departure. However, Louis remained very unpopular with the people of France.

In February 1815, Napoleon starting from the south, moved north towards Paris. The French people were on his side and he was successful in re-recruiting his former troops and veterans along the way. After meeting some resistance the French troops failed to attack him, disobeying commanding orders and switched sides to their former Emperor. He arrived in Paris on 22 March 1815, after King Louis XVIII had fled north to Belgium. Napoleon took power in Paris, reinstating his loyal leaders.

War

Napoleon realised that he had to take on the allies, including the Dutch, and the Prussian military leader Marshall Blücher, as they were determined to get rid of him. There were two armies: the Prussians led by Blücher and the allies led by the Duke of Wellington.

Battle of Waterloo A Short Account

Gebhard Leberecht von Blücher

ll Marshall Blücher

Belgium

In June 1815, Napoleon marched to Belgium where the allies were gathered, with 20,000 British infantry, believing that the Austrian and Prussian armies would take some time to get to the French border.

Duke of Wellington

III Duke of Wellington

Field Marshal Arthur Wellesley, 1st Duke of Wellington

The Duke of Wellington had confidence in the British Infantry. However the Duke was unsure and had less confidence in the British Cavalry, as they tended to be unruly and wasn't certain that he would be able to recall them, once they had been deployed.

Lord Uxbridge, Marquise of Anglesey

IV Henry Paget, 2nd Earl of Uxbridge

Lord Uxbridge, Marquise of Anglesey had eloped with the Duke of Wellington's Sister-in-law, however was one of the Duke's good military commanders.

Prussian Army

The Prussian Army was made up mostly of regular line infantry, who had been fighting for two to three years. They were renowned for having fought doggedly.

French Army

The French Army, Armée du Nord, was the name given to the forces commanded by Napoleon. It contained 130,000 infantry, as well as many cavalry and artillery units. Morale was brittle, as the troops had shown disloyalty to King Louis XVIII, and had switched allegiances, making commanders wonder whether they would do so again.

Betrayal was a part of this fragility, as prior to the battle of Waterloo, on 15

Battle of Waterloo A Short Account

Jun 1815, a French General rode to the enemy with the entire battle plans for the French.

Marshall Ney commanded the French left wing and Marshall Grouchy commanded the right French wing.

Battle of Waterloo A Short Account

Emmanuel de Grouchy, 2ème Marquis de Grouchy

V Marshall Grouchy

Jean-de-Dieu Soult

VI Jean-de-Dieu Soult

Napoleon appointed Marshall Soult as the field commander, Major-general and chief of staff. Soult was not a good choice of Commander of Staff as he failed to keep a tight rein on what was going on.

Conflict

Napoleon made his move earlier than the Duke of Wellington expected.

The Duchess of Richmond held a ball the night before the battle on 15 June 1815, so the senior commanders spent the evening beforehand at the ball.

Battle of Waterloo A Short Account

Duchess of Richmond

VII Charlotte Lennox, Duchess of Richmond née Lady Charlotte Gordon

The Ridge

The battle began on 16 June 1815 in fields in Belgium adjacent to a long ridge running east-west, perpendicular to, and bisected by, the main road to Brussels. Wellington used the ridge as cover for the allied troops making certain they were outside of the line of sight of the French Artillery.

Battle of Quatre Bras

Napoleon tactics was to split the allies in two. Troops were marched to the crossroads at Quatre Bras. The battle was referred to as like being 'conducted on a pocket handkerchief'.

The French Marshall Ney found the crossroads of Quatre Bras was held by the Prince of Orange. Initial attacks were repelled. However, significant numbers of French troops soon overwhelmed them.

Wellington arrived and took command. He successfully drove Marshall Ney and the French troops back, re-securing the crossroads, by early evening.

This was too late to go to the aid of the Prussians who were also in battle with the French Cavalry.

Battle of Ligny

Napoleon first attacked the Prussians who had arrived. The Prussians stood and fought, despite being surrounded on two sides. It was a tough fight. They were mauled by the French Cavalry, despite forming squares, making it hard for the cavalry's lances to break into the square formations of those on foot.

The centre gave way under the French assaults and Blücher's Prussians were defeated, although the flanks continued to hold their ground.

Marshall Blücher was unseated from his horse during the battle and still survived, despite being surrounded by the French.

The Prussian defeat at the 'Battle of Ligny,' was the last victory by

Napoleon. The defeat made Wellington's position at Quatre Bras untenable. Wellington withdrew northwards on the 17 June, taking up a more defensive position behind the low ridge of Mont-Saint Jean, located south of the village of Waterloo and the adjacent Sonian Forest.

Battle of Waterloo A Short Account

August Neidhardt von Gneisenau

VIII August Neidhardt von Gneisenau Prussian Chief of Staff

August Neidhardt von Gneisenau was the Prussian Chief of Staff. He ordered a retreat and went north, staying in touch with the allies. Napoleon believed otherwise and thought that the Prussians had retreated east towards their homeland.

Thunderstorm

On the night of 17 June there was a thunderstorm with torrential rain, soaking the ground and exposing the men to the wet weather.

Battle of Waterloo A Short Account

Alexander Cavalié Mercer

IX Alexander Cavalié Mercer

Alexander Cavalié Mercer was the commander of G Troop British Royal Horse Artillery. They arrived too late for the battle of Quatre Bras.

His troop had left England for Belgium on 11 April 1815. He fought with the cavalry rear-guard, which covered the allies retreat to the field of Waterloo. He spent the night of the thunderstorm miserable and hungry, waded deep in mud at Mont-Saint Jean farm.

Napoleon marched north to Waterloo and is believed to have been seen bathed in sunlight with a small group on horseback.

Mercer's troops came under heavy fire against superior French artillery, before retiring, as they found themselves exposed in front of the allies, who were on the ridge behind them.

La Belle Alliance

La Belle Alliance Inn on the morning of 18 June 1815, became the headquarters for Napoleon, prior to the Battle of Waterloo.

The inn was also the place where the Duke of Wellington and Marshall Blücher met at around 21:00 on 18 June 1815, after the Battle of Waterloo.

La Haye Sainte

La Haye Sainte is a walled farmhouse compound and was initially captured by the French, giving them a defensible position against the allies, and was part of Napoleon's strategy of trying to tear the allies apart, and in particular breaking Wellington's line of defence.

Hougoumont

Château d'Hougoumont was a large farmhouse, near Waterloo. The nearby escarpment is where allied forces faced Napoleon's Army at the Battle of Waterloo on Sunday 18 June 1815. Many allies were garrisoned there and it was fortified, making it a key target for Napoleon.

The walls were high and had platforms behind, so that the allies could defend the property.

The French couldn't get over the walls, as they had no ladders, despite making several attempts.

Private Clay was caught outside of the property and the French took several pot shots, trying to kill him, however he managed to survive and eventually was let in through a door.

Hougoumont's North Gate was breached by the French with an axe wielded by Sous-Lieutenant Legros.

Five allied officers fought to shut the gate successfully.

All thirty French troops were killed who got in following fierce hand to hand fighting, with only a drummer boy surviving.

The garrison was running low on ammunition. An ammunition cart was successfully driven through the French lines, resupplying the troops.

Coordinated cavalry attacks continued against the allied troops behind Hougoumont, with the fighting continuing around the property all afternoon.

Also Napoleon personally ordered the shelling of the house. Everything, except the chapel, was badly damaged by fire, however the British line was held and the French didn't succeed in breaking the line.

The Duke of Wellington is reputed to have said later that day, "*The success of the battle turned upon the closing of the gates at Hougoumont.*"

Battle of Waterloo A Short Account

Jean-Baptiste Drouet, Comte d'Erlon

X Jean-Baptiste Drouet, Comte d'Erlon

At 13:30 on 18 June d'Erlon Corps attacked the Allied centre near La Haye Sainte in Column formation. His advance was stopped by Picton's

Peninsular War veterans. Then the British heavy cavalry attacked his corps' flanks. He retreated with the rest of the French army.

Thomas Picton

XI Lieutenant General Sir Thomas Picton

Lieutenant General Sir Thomas Picton was a Welsh British Army officer. Picton's division stopped d'Erlon's corps' attack and he was the most senior officer to be killed at Waterloo. He was shot in the forehead and fell from his horse.

Napoleon at the Ridge

XII Napoléon Bonaparte

The French advanced and gained the ridge and in doing so thought that they had won. However the British Infantry was waiting in line, let off a quick volley and then in close proximity to the French charged with bayonets, forcing the French back to the ridge's hedges. The Union Brigade and the Household Brigade attacked the French and swept them away.

Charge of the Royal Scots Greys

The Royal Scots Greys were positioned as the third line of defence and held in reserve.

Lieutenant-Colonel Hamilton ordered the Royal Scots Greys, which he was commanding, forward at the walk, because of the sodden ground. Their arrival on the scene helped to rally the other British brigades, who had begun to wane. They began cutting the French Infantry to pieces.

Once the French Battle standard had been captured, the Scots Greys continued their advance and galloped toward the next infantry division. Some of the infantry had time to form their defensive squares, which the Scots were unable to break.

The Scots Greys, as feared by Wellington, forgot their supporting role and ignored the recall.

Capture of the French Eagle

Sergeant Charles Ewart of the Royal Scots Greys, with much daring, captured the French Battle Standard Eagle, belonging to the 45th French Regiment of the Line.

Battle of Waterloo A Short Account

Major-General Sir William Ponsonby

XIII Major-General Sir William Ponsonby

Major-General Sir William Ponsonby was commander of the Union Brigade.

Following successful counter attacks, the brigade failed to rally. They continued towards the French positions, charging in disordered groups, resulting in their horses being blown up by the French guns, followed by swift retribution from French Lancers.

Consequently, they and the Royal Scots Greys brigades suffered very heavy losses, eliminating them from any further action in the battle.

Ponsonby became isolated among the French, and was killed along with other unseated similar cavalry men.

The French Cavalry

At 16:00 the French think that the British Cavalry is in retreat.

Marshall Ney leads the French up to the ridge and finds that the allies' infantry are deployed in squares and are successful in keeping the French out. The French Cavalry attack continues for a couple of hours, until the French cavalry retreat to allow bombardment of the enemy.

The Square

An infantry square, is a combat formation, so that infantry form in close order, to repel a cavalry attack. A whole battalion constructs themselves, into a hollow square. The sides were composed of two or more ranks of soldiers armed with single-shot guns with fixed bayonets. In the centre the commander and standard were positioned, together with a reserve force, as back-up as needed.

The infantry would volley fire at approaching cavalry, waiting until they were within 20 to 30 metres. Horses and dead bodies would form further protection to attack.

Discipline was needed to retain the formation and protection for all, especially the timing of the volley. It allows for one cavalry man on horse to come up against four infantry men in any situation, facilitating a combined attack by the infantry.

Brest plate

French Heavy Cavalrymen wore armour on the battlefield, together with white leather riding pants and black riding boots that extended past the knee.

Antoine Favreau served as one of Napoleon's heavy cavalrymen and would have gleamed in the light with his breast plate. The breast plate he was wearing failed to save his life, as a cannon ball pierced the armour.

Battle of Waterloo A Short Account

Horses will not charge into the line of bayonets.

Michel Ney

XIV Michel Ney, 1st Duc d'Elchingen, 1st Prince de la Moskowa

Michel Ney, 1st Duc d'Elchingen and 1st Prince de la Moskowa, was Napoleon's second in command. He misinterpreted the redeployment of the allied troops to be that of a retreat, rather than a re-grouping. In this belief, Ney ordered the French Cavalry to charge the allies.

The ground was saturated when the French cavalry charged down the ridge, across the valley and up the opposite ridge to a plateau, where they met the enemy infantry formed in squares.

The charge was broken and the men were picked off. Ney should have realised that the ground was too sodden to reach a full charge, He kept sending in the cavalry, depleting resources.

Napoleon ordered Marshall Ney to capture La Haye Sainte. He failed to do so, as his attention was diverted with the cavalry attacks.

About 18:30 the French Marshall Ney, captured La Haye Sainte with a furious assault, as the light battalion of the German Legion had expended all its ammunition, and retreated. Following this achievement, the French deployed their canons devastatingly close to the Anglo-Allied lines.

The final assault

Wellington's centre had been exposed by the fall of La Haye Sainte.

At 19:00 the French from La Haye Sainte climbed the escarpment to attack the Allies. The French attack was beaten back.

The Prussians arrived from the east. Napoleon conned his troops by telling them that they were French reinforcements.

The fighting was very tough in the village of Waterloo. At a range of 300 yards, the French artillery was brutal. Those that surrendered were slaughtered without mercy on both sides.

Wellington's men suffered heavily from the bombardment.

The 27th Inniskilling Regiment, an Irish infantry regiment of the British Army, in coming to the aid of other infantry, were attacked by the French Cavalry.

The 698 men strong battalion, was deployed in square formation, at the crossroads of Ohain Road and the Charleroi to Brussels highway.

There were 478 casualties, within a very short time. By 20:10 the French had been routed. During the French retreat, La Haye Sainte was quickly recaptured by the Allies.

The Rout

The Prussian Army deployed on both sides of the village. Wellington brought up fresh units.

Napoleon committed his last reserve of the Imperial Guard. Napoleon's intension was to break through Wellington's centre.

After Napoleon made a speech to inspire his troops, he oversaw the deployment himself, ensuring two batteries of Imperial Guard Horse Artillery strengthen the Imperial Guard.

Napoleon instructed Ney to conduct the assault. Ney failed to achieve what Napoleon had ordered, of attacking straight up the centre.

The battle between the best of the British raged, against the best of the French divisions.

The British laid down in the tall corn fields and attacked the French at close-quarter, surprising the French with a wall of red uniforms of Soldiers that appeared, firing a volley.

Sir Peregrine Maitland

XV General Sir Peregrine Maitland

Battle of Waterloo A Short Account

The British General Sir Peregrine Maitland, who had served with distinction at the Battle Quatre Bras, told the troops "*Now is your time*".

The French ran.

Maitland succeeded in repelling the final French assault, of the French Imperial Guard.

In the attacks, the Dutch Prince of Orange was seriously wounded.

The timely arrival of the Dutch General Chassé, turned the tide in favour of the allies. Many French deserted from their ranks. They had been broken.

The 52nd Oxfordshire Light Infantry Regiment, outflanked the Imperial Guard successfully, attacking the Imperial Guard flank with fire.

Wellington and the allied generals advanced with the remnants of their artillery forces.

The last square of the Imperial Old Guard refused to surrender choosing death, in the smoke and darkness of the last efforts and hours, of the fighting in the battle.

The retreating allied troops were surrounded by thousands of fleeing French troops, running for the French border.

The coalition cavalry harried the fugitives until about 23:00.

The Prussian Chief-of-Staff Gneisenau pursued them as far as Genappe, before he ordered a halt to the pursuit of Napoleon, who escaped capture.

The Duke of Wellington declared that it had been a *'close run thing'*, in his meeting at the Inn with Marshall Blücher, late evening of Sunday 18 June 1815. Wellington said that if the Prussians hadn't turned up, "*it would have been a different outcome*".

Casualties

The whole area was strewn with corpses, casualties, wounded and men suffering from a lack of water over the one and a quarter square miles, over which the Battle of Waterloo had occurred.

Throughout the night there was much stepping over bodies and plundering. Those still alive were knifed for their possessions and valuables, including clothing.

The following day tourists from nearby, visited the battlefield to gawp, experiencing the stench of death, blood, destruction and carnage.

The death count amounted to some 40,000 bodies and 16,000 horses, making the Battle of Waterloo a very bloody conflict. It brought the war against Napoleon that had been raging for 22 years, to an end.

Asylum

Being unable to escape from the Prussian's pursuit of him, Napoleon demanded asylum from the British Captain Frederick Maitland on HMS Bellerophon on 15 July 1815.

Napoleon surrendered himself to Maitland and in French announced "*I am come to throw myself on the protection of your Prince and your laws.*" Maitland bowed in acceptance of Napoleons' plea.

With the former emperor in custody aboard a British warship, the Napoleonic Wars were finally over.

The British kept Napoleon prisoner, on the Island of Saint Helena in the Atlantic Ocean, until he died on 5 May 1821.

HMS Bellerophon

XVI HMS Bellerophon

HMS Bellerophon was paid off and converted to a prison ship in 1815, and subsequently renamed Captivity.

The ship was moored off Plymouth, Devon for two weeks in July 1815, with Napoleon on Board, whilst the authorities came to a decision about what to do with him.

On 31 July 1815, the authorities communicated to Napoleon their decision to make him a prisoner on

Battle of Waterloo A Short Account

the remote Island of St. Helena, in the South Atlantic Ocean.

Battle of Waterloo A Short Account

About Felicity McCullough

Felicity McCullough has a wide variety of interests and has been taking photographs for many years and she has published some of her photographs in bite-sized glimpses in her series '*Places to Visit*'.

This brief account of the Battle of Waterloo is her first in the series '*Glimpses of the Past*' and compliments Places to Visit.

Felicity painted the portraits of the illustrations in the book, from looking at a range of images recorded of the individuals mentioned, and consequently they may not be a true likeness.

Books in the series: *Places to Visit*: -

> Chester A Photographic Glimpse
>
> Newton Abbot A Photographic Glimpse

Other Publications

Additionally, Felicity McCullough has written several books about '*Preventative Health Care*' for goats. The website www.goatlapshop.com has a wide variety of topics and resources that relate to goats, including other guides in the '*Goat Knowledge Series*'.

The '*Charlie And Isabella's Magical Adventures*' Series of Children's Books, about the adventures of two magical goats, which are suitable for bedtime reading and are beautifully illustrated, are also available from the Publisher My Lap Shop Publishers.

Index

27th Inniskilling Regiment, 44
52nd Oxfordshire Light Infantry Regiment, 47
Allies, 12, 13, 22, 26, 28, 29, 39, 42, 43, 44, 47
Armée du Nord, 16
Austria, 9
Austrian, 14
Ball, 20, 40
Battle of Ligny, 23
Battle of Waterloo, 1, 4, 10, 28, 29, 49, 53
Belgium, 12, 13, 21, 28
Blücher, 12, 13, 23, 29, 48
Breast plate, 40
Britain, 9, 10
British Army, 33, 44
British Cavalry, 15, 39
British infantry, 14
British Royal Horse Artillery, 27
Brussels, 22, 44
Casualties, 44, 48
Charleroi, 44
Chief of Staff, 25
Coalition, 4, 10, 48
Death count, 49
d'Erlon, 32, 33
Duchess of Richmond, 20, 21
Duke of Wellington, 12, 14, 15, 16, 20, 28, 31, 48

Dutch, 12, 47
Elba, 9
Ewart, 36
France, 4, 9, 10, 11
French, 9, 10, 12, 14, 16, 17, 22, 23, 28, 29, 30, 31, 33, 35, 36, 38, 39, 40, 42, 43, 44, 45, 47, 48, 50
French Army, 16
French Artillery, 22
French border, 14, 48
French Cavalry, 23, 39, 44
French Lancers, 38
Genappe, 48
German Legion, 43
Gneisenau, 25, 48
Grouchy, 17
HMS Bellerophon, 50, 51
Horse Artillery, 45
Hougoumont, 29, 30, 31
Imperial Guard, 45, 47
La Belle Alliance, 28
La Haye Sainte, 29, 32, 42, 43, 44
Louis 18th, 11
Maitland, 46, 47, 50
McCullough, 1, 53
Mercer, 27, 28
Mont-Saint Jean, 28
Mont-Saint-Jean, 24
My Lap Shop Publishers, 2, 3, 54, 59
Napoleonic Wars, 9, 50
Netherlands, 9

Ney, 17, 22, 39, 41, 42, 45
Ohain Road, 44
Old Guard, 47
Paris, 9, 12
Plymouth, 2, 3, 51, 59
Ponsonby, 37, 38
Portugal, 9
Prince of Orange, 22, 47
Private Clay, 30
Prussia, 9
Prussian Army, 16, 45
Prussians, 9, 12, 23, 26, 43, 48
Quatre Bras, 22, 24, 27, 47
Ridge, 22, 24, 28, 35, 39, 42
Royal Scots Greys, 35, 36, 38
Russia, 9
Saint Helena, 50
Sardinia, 9
Sonian Forest, 24
Soult, 19
Sous-Lieutenant Legros, 30
Spain, 9
Square, 23, 39, 44, 47, 49
Sweden, 9
Thomas Picton, 33
Thunderstorm, 26, 28
Uxbridge, 15, 16
Waterloo, 9, 16, 24, 28, 29, 34, 43

Battle of Waterloo A Short Account

Published by:

My Lap Shop Publishers

91 Mayflower Street, Unit 222,
Plymouth, Devon PL1 1SB,
United Kingdom
Tel: +44 (0)871 560 5297
www.mylapshop.com

About My Lap Shop Publishers

First Edition June 2015

www.ingramcontent.com/pod-product-compliance
Lightning Source LLC
Chambersburg PA
CBHW071758040426
42446CB00012B/2616